Rain Riding Techniques

A Practical Guide To Wet Weather Motorcycle Riding

Todd Thompson

Copyright © 2005 by Todd Thompson

All rights reserved. No part of this book shall be reproduced or transmitted in any form or by any means, electronic, mechanical, magnetic, photographic including photocopying, recording or by any information storage and retrieval system, without prior written permission of the publisher. No patent liability is assumed with respect to the use of the information contained herein. Although every precaution has been taken in the preparation of this book, the publisher and author assume no responsibility for errors or omissions. Neither is any liability assumed for damages resulting from the use of the information contained herein.

ISBN 0-7414-2695-1

Published by:

INFINITY
PUBLISHING.COM

1094 New DeHaven Street, Suite 100
West Conshohocken, PA 19428-2713
Info@buybooksontheweb.com
www.buybooksontheweb.com
Toll-free (877) BUY BOOK
Local Phone (610) 941-9999
Fax (610) 941-9959

Printed in the United States of America

Printed on Recycled Paper

Published September 2005

Acknowledgments

I'd like to thank my wife, Mary, for taking her time to contribute her riding expertise and support in editing this book. I'd also like to thank my good friend Bob Collin for contributing his assistance and riding expertise. Bob, I trust your 5th Maine to Alaska ride is going well and you're dry and warm.

I am fortunate to be a close relative of Mr. Herb Gunnison. Herb is one of motorcycling's living legends. With over seventy years of on and off road riding under his belt, he has kindly passed on his rain riding and editing experience to help make this book possible. Thanks Herb. I don't travel any road in the United States or Canada without thinking you've already been here, done that.

Mary at Briar Island, Nova Scotia, July 2004

Down Digby Neck and two ferry boats later we were here in all the fog. The rain came soon after. Nova Scotia and its people are simply the best!

Table of Contents

Chapter 1: Introduction 1

Chapter 2: The Mind of the Wet Weather Rider 7

Chapter 3: Some Riding Techniques 15

Chapter 4: Introduction to Wet Braking 21

Chapter 5: Wet Weather Traction 25

Chapter 6: Highway Versus Byways: 29

Chapter 7: Rush Hour in the Rain 37

Chapter 8: To Continue or Stop When the Rain Starts? 41

Chapter 9: Highway Toll Booths… 47

Chapter 10: Being Seen / Protective Gear 53

Chapter 11: A Few Quick Words on Clothing 57

Chapter 12: Final Thoughts 61

Chapter 1

Introduction

When I was a pre-teen, we had an outdoor summer play toy called a "Slip & Slide". It was a piece of plastic maybe 4 feet wide by 25 feet long. We would flood this with water and then, running with all our might, we could slide the length of it as if we were on Teflon. What fun!

For many motorcyclists without rain riding experience, the thought of riding a motorcycle in the rain is tantamount to running down a Slip & Slide. Many riders cannot relax for fear of dropping the bike on the first tight corner or when having to apply their brakes on a rain soaked road. They fear sliding down the street like on my childhood Slip and Slide. However, as you gain rain riding experience, you will be able to relax – yes, even enjoy riding in the rain.

Many motorcycle riders shy away from wet weather riding. There are a number of reasons for this such as:

- Lack of physical comfort.
- Mental stress while riding in the rain.
- Simply don't like the idea of getting wet.
- Perceived lack of control in the event of hard braking or an emergency maneuver.

With today's tire technology, motorcycles are safely controllable on wet pavement. And with today's rain gear, riding can be a dry and comfortable outing.

There are many terrific books that discuss riding techniques and street survival. Here are two I believe are worth reading:

- David Hough's, <u>Proficient Motorcyling Techniques</u>, offers the beginning and experienced rider tips and methods of everyday riding survival.
- Nick Ienatsch's, <u>Sport Riding Techniques,</u> offers a truly terrific tutorial on mastering motorcycle control for street and racing riders.

I am an advocate of reading both these books and others and then practicing what you read. You can never learn enough about our fantastic sport.

We should never become so complacent that we forget the inherent risks we assume for the right and joy of riding motorcycles. Take a motorcycling beginner, refresher and or experienced rider course. Practice the throttle and braking techniques you learn from riding courses and from reading books.

If you've avoided riding in the rain, why not plan an outing with an experienced rain rider? Or, visit a nearby parking lot on a rainy day to hone your braking and throttle skills. This is always a worthwhile activity and one that should be practiced repeatedly. Besides, it's a lot of fun and will pay back dividends when you're back out on the street.

Take the time to talk to seasoned riders. Ask them what riding tips they have acquired over the years of rain riding. Without the benefit of experienced people and their knowledge, new and seasoned riders may have a tough and potentially painful time acquiring good rain riding skills. This book will explore some of these rain riding techniques which will, hopefully, allow you to ride whenever and wherever you want.

Rain Riding Techniques

Before we move on, we should detail several motorcycle control skills in case this is the first and only book you have read on riding techniques. Understanding these terms will help you to better understand the techniques we are discussing in this book.

- **Compression braking**: Your ability to use engine compression braking, (rolling off the throttle partially or entirely to slow down), is diminished in wet weather. On dry pavement you might be able to slam the throttle shut without skidding the rear tire. This may not be possible on wet pavement. Also on dry pavement, you may be able to down shift directly into 3rd gear from 5th at 45 mph without momentarily locking up the rear wheel, depending on the bike you're riding. On wet pavement this may cause a nasty rear wheel skid and loss of control. Learning to "blip" the throttle to increase rpm's while down shifting will minimize the possibility of locking up the rear wheel and losing traction and also allow compression braking.

- **Throttle maintenance**: This is a technique of keeping the front and rear tires at equal traction by maintaining your throttle at even power. Rolling off the throttle abruptly can transfer weight to the front wheel while un-weighting the rear wheel to the extent that you can lose rear wheel traction completely. Conversely "throttle loading" by accelerating hard, loads the rear wheel and causes the front tire to lose traction, as you might in accelerating around and out of a corner. The front tire can skid out leaving you struggling for control or lying on the street as target for the cars in front and behind you. Using throttle maintenance allows the bike to neither accelerate nor decelerate drastically (as in compression breaking) in the turn. Therefore, the bike's chassis is not stressed and the bike will maintain its composure.

3

- **Trail braking** is the technique of adding just a tad of rear braking while in a turn to decrease your speed continuously and therefore decrease the needed lean angle to execute the turn. Adding "maintenance throttle" during a turn and using trail braking is a good way to maintain traction balance on the front and rear tires while slowing down to negotiate a turn. This is a very effective technique to master and can keep you out of harm's way on a rain soaked or dry road. While trail braking, be aware of the front wheel wanting to tuck in if your speed is too high. This is one sign of an eminent low side. You'll first feel it in the handle bars. Begin practicing light braking at moderate speed and lean angles to get used to how your bike behaves while braking in a turn.

For more information on these motorcycle control techniques and topics, read the books I referenced before. Certainly, these aren't the only books on the subjects. Check with your dealer, favorite bookstore or Internet to see what books are available. There are lots to choose from. Some are better than others but almost all have something valuable to teach.

Ultimately, the decision to ride in wet weather or not is yours. Your success in riding safely in the rain will depend upon your ability to maintain traction, plan for potential accident escape routes, control braking and throttle properly, and assess the riding environment correctly.

This book offers a few techniques and lessons that will help you ride more safely and enjoyably in the rain. I do not guarantee that if you employ these techniques, you will always have a safe ride. Your degree of success will depend upon your mental state, your control skills and your decision to ride versus "sitting this one out". I and most skilled riders believe that safe motorcycling is 90% mental and 10% physical preparation. Keeping out of harm's way is all about screwing your head on correctly before swinging your leg over the saddle.

Believe it or not, this is a paved local road in Connecticut. After a hard rain the road was covered with mud runoff. It was very slippery. Can you imagine coming upon this after a blind corner?

Herb Gunnison, put the joy of rain riding succinctly for me in his book, Seventy Years on a Motorcycle,

> *Oh how I love to ride on drizzly summer days tucked in behind a misty windscreen, insulated from the moist wind chill by a rain suit, listening to the song of a well tuned engine, absorbed in the rush of my solitary world – lonely, unassailable, aching with day-long joy as I watch the earth renew itself around me.*

Chapter 2

The Mind of the Wet Weather Rider

Rain riders are patient. Rain riders are thinkers. And they continuously do the following things:

1. Evaluate:

A patient rider takes the time to evaluate the current condition of the roadway. They ask the questions:

- How much traffic has passed since it last rained? Is this road heavily traveled (like an interstate) with many trucks and cars?
- How many days has it been since it last rained? How much oil has accumulated over the past rainless period? This will give you a good indication of the oil build up over time on the road.
- Has this slippery mess had a chance to wash off? Have the cars and trucks had adequate time to wash the oils off the road or not?
- What will my available traction and braking limits be on this road at this moment?

Knowing when it last rained will help you to **estimate** your available tire traction. Please note, I said **estimate**. Nothing in life is ever guaranteed, especially tire traction.

Having answers to these questions will enable you to evaluate riding conditions and take steps to ride more safely and comfortably. Just like riding on dry roads, riding safely on wet roads is a combination of road, traffic and speed evaluations with the proper use of brakes and throttle.

2. Relax:

In the event of rain, you should first slow down and stay relaxed. A relaxed rider will always fare better than a tense rider. A relaxed rider is able to think. A thinking rider will be able to apply throttle and braking control techniques more smoothly than a tense rider. A tense rider will usually react in a "knee jerk" manner, like grabbing a fist and foot full of brakes resulting in a "low side" slide* down the street. Rain riding is about mastering your brake and throttle control. Knowing how much throttle and or brake pressure you can apply on a dry surface versus wet is your key to wet weather survival. Master your *total* throttle control, including throttle braking and throttle roll-on.

* A "low side" slide is when the motorcycle loses traction and slides down the street on it's side while you exit low off the bike. Although low sides are scary, you can usually walk, maybe limp away from one.

Note: Most experienced riders advocate that once in a committed low side it's best to continue the slide and not release the rear brake. The risk of injury by inadvertently entering into a high side is far riskier than injury in a low side. You are more likely to encounter serious injuries from a high side than you are from a low side exit off the bike.

This shows a road covered with sand after a hard summer rain. Some people call this type of rain a gulley washer. Makes sense because the sand came from the road gullies on either side. After a gully washer, slow down and take it easy when turning or braking on these roads.

3. Practice:

Practice mastering front and rear wheel braking, counter steering, and weight shift techniques to maintain total control of your motorcycle. You should be able to combine all these disciplines in a coordinated and smoothly controlled manner on all roads – wet or dry.

Many of you have taken a Motorcycling Safety Foundation (MSF) course. Hopefully, you've been practicing the art of throttle and braking control. Controlling a motorcycle in dry weather presents many challenges for us. Wet weather compounds these challenges. If you haven't mastered these disciplines on dry pavement don't try them on wet. You'll only be asking for trouble and maybe a trip to the hospital and most likely to the bank to fix your broken motorcycle. Practice makes perfect. Perfect your braking technique on dry pavement and then test your available traction on wet pavement – preferably in a large lonely parking lot with a friend to watch over you.

The first time I rode during a substantial rain storm I was with a group of very experienced riders. Although I had practiced my wet braking in a local parking lot, I was very nervous. Following the more experienced riders was a great way to introduce me to road rain riding. I had made them aware that I was a novice rain rider. They slowed more than usual to keep me safe and comfortable. I had the opportunity to imitate their riding, speed and braking techniques. This really improved my rain riding confidence. Next time it rains, ask an experience rider to go with you and lead the way.

4. Slow down:

When riding in wet weather, it is important to put all you do into slower motion. This means you counter steer a bit more slowly, brake sooner and throttle up and down more slowly. Remember, your tires will have less grip on a wet road.

5. Plan:

Become the thinking rider. If you have a time schedule that must be kept and you anticipate wet weather, you should adjust your schedule while you adjust your riding technique. Keeping a dry weather riding schedule in wet weather will make for a tense and potentially dangerous ride. It also leads to fatigue and frustration. Your chances for an accident increase dramatically. Decisions become hard and more delayed. Your speed can become more erratic and your ability to anticipate becomes compromised. There's just simply no fun in that. Develop a wet weather head for wet weather riding. Plan where you need to be at any given moment on the road should a traffic situation arise. Plan your escapes, your passes, and develop your "What if's?" all the time. Generally, I build a wet weather time schedule even though the forecast is calling for fantastic weather my entire trip. Ask yourself, "How often is the weather man 100% right? "

6. Stay aware:

The wet weather rider is an aware rider. In rainy conditions, it is up to you to plan your moves and escape routes continuously. You cannot trust other drivers around you to do the logical thing. In wet weather you will also have to scan traffic more closely. You will have to focus to the sides, the rear and farther down the road to see potential problems or concerns. This becomes quite a feat considering that your own visibility maybe reduced in rain.

7. Ensure clear visibility and being visible

Visibility can be a real challenge when passing trucks and their tire spray. Think ahead. Anticipate where you need to be in traffic to stay safe – out of harm's way. Maneuver smartly. Stay as far left as you safely can when passing vehicles in the rain.

If your vision is very restricted, it may be prudent to pull off the road and let the rain subside or wait until it stops. Being a patient rider here may prove to be the right move.

Rain riders typically have clothing that is highly reflective at night and brightly colored during the day. Wearing a reflective florescent vest is a very good way to make sure traffic sees you. See chapter 10 for a bit more on this.

> **Tip: Keeping a dry weather time table for a wet weather ride is asking for trouble and possible injury.**

In summary:

1. Practice wet weather braking and throttle control in a nearby parking lot.

2. Become the thinking rider, a patient rider. Evaluate the local climate, the road and traffic conditions all the time.

3. Have escape routes planned to evacuate without incident the lane or highway if you need to.

4. Wear brightly colored clothes or reflective gear to improve the chances of being seen by other drivers.

5. Take a Rider Course – frequently to ensure skill maintenance.

Rain Riding Techniques

Luckily these trucks were on this side of the curve. Coming around the corner at full speed and finding them blindly is not something for the faint of heart or on a rainy day. There were no traffic managers to assist us. If you look carefully you can see the car passing the 1st truck on the left side. We could not see oncoming traffic during this maneuver. We proceeded very cautiously.

Chapter 3

Some Riding Techniques

The skilled wet weather rider continuously evaluates the weather and road conditions. Ask yourself, "Has enough time elapsed (since the last rain) for a significant build up of oil and grease to provide a slippery surface?" If 1 week or more has elapsed since the last rain then you can bet that the road surface will float an oily film when the rain starts. This time span depends on the volume of traffic. The more traffic, the less time it will take to build up a significant layer of oil. Remember, *oil floats on water*. Tires don't grip well on road oil and grease.

When rain first begins, we should take the time to evaluate the road surface. Decide if it is prudent to wait 30 minutes or more for accumulated oil and grease to float off the road surface. On the other hand, if it rained for 3 days, 12 hours ago then the road might be relatively clean of oils. Your available tire grip might be pretty good.

The skilled rain rider continuously evaluates the weather. Scan the direction in which you are riding. Get to know your cloud formations so you can spot brewing storms and approaching rain.

1. Is a front approaching and how fast?
2. Are the clouds thickening and or darkening?
3. Is the wind picking up?
4. Does the oncoming traffic consistently have their lights on?
5. Is the oncoming traffic using their wipers?

Answering yes to these questions tells you that you may be in for a soaker. Putting on the rain gear before getting soaked will keep you comfortable and dry. Anticipate the weather if you can.

One of the most important rain riding skills to develop is to know when to **slow down**. I have a friend who says: "the secret to wet weather riding is 80%". He rides in wet weather by doing everything at 80 % of dry weather riding. This means that, as a general rule, he rides at 80% of his usual speed and applies 80% of the braking pedal pressures he would apply on dry pavement.

Running 80% is a good idea but this simple percentage technique doesn't account for one's need to evaluate the road conditions that I spoke of before. Maybe the road conditions dictate applying 70%, 50% or even less. Experienced riders continuously evaluate the road conditions and their weather environment as they proceed.

A Wet Weather Lesson:

Sometimes, wet weather riding comes in surprise forms. I was on my way to San Diego. It was a moonless night. Somewhere outside of El Centro, California, I encountered what I thought was light rain. The trucks were sending the rain up as tire spray. Visibility was reduced. I slowed down, concerned, not knowing when it had last rained. I had just come from Abilene, TX. I thought about stopping to put on my rain gear. It was in the high 60's. I looked up to check the cloud cover and saw, to my amazement, stars! This wasn't rain! It was dew, really heavy dew. The lesson here is that even on a clear cloudless night you can encounter wet riding conditions. This is something to remember.

Other riding techniques:

- Take a riding break, letting the passing traffic wash the road clean of oils and grease.

- Ride in the tire tracks of the cars and trucks ahead of you.

- Stay clear of the oil and debris covered center groove. Try not to ride down the center of any lane. Move to either side of the lane (the tire tracks in each lane). You can actually see the oil build-up as evidenced by the darker color stripe running down the middle of the lane. This is especially true on freeways and interstates.

- Don't travel in the far right lanes if you can possibly avoid them. I spend the bulk of my time in the far left lane on a multilane highway.

Don't forget that in the rain, you should be relaxed and aware of all traffic, road hazards and the weather in front, to the sides and in back of you. Know where your weather is coming from. It makes a huge difference if the storm is moving in from the side, versus the front or behind. Your riding style will change based on the direction of the storm winds. Plan and maneuver to avoid being placed in harm's way. Plan your escape routes ahead of time. The last thing you want to be doing during a traffic panic attack is to be looking for an escape route. You should have one or two planned long before.

> **Tip: take 800mg of Ibuprofen before long rides. This will help to cut down on inflammation of your muscles and joints.**
>
> **Do active and isometric exercises while riding to improve circulation and by wearing support stockings. Make sure Smokey isn't behind you. He may pull you over to see what the heck you're doing. Maybe you should first pull into a rest area?**

In summary:

1. Slow down.
2. Evaluate the road, the traffic and the weather. Ask yourself: Will this rain last long? Is the road clean of oils or have they built up over a long rainless period? When did it last rain?
3. Brake carefully applying the front first and then the rear.
4. Monitor the traffic and plan escape routes.
5. Maintain ample distance between you and the car in front so you won't have to make any panic moves.
6. If you encounter a thunderstorm, wait in a sheltered area until the initial winds die down, then proceed.
7. Stay out of the far right lane if possible.
8. Stay out if the center (oily) track of any lane of possible.
9. Know where your changing weather is coming from.
10. Relax, enjoy the ride.

Rain Riding Techniques

This is not a right turn you want to negotiate in a panic. See the sand? If you miss the turn continue up the road and turn around. Continuously evaluating the road surface can keep you from having a nasty accident and injury.

Chapter 4

Introduction to Wet Braking

Get to know your rear and front brake intimately on dry pavement first before exploring the braking envelopes in wet weather. If you haven't mastered using the rear brake without a lock up in dry weather then you should practice. Practice until you have achieved the shortest stopping distance for any given speed.

- Start by traveling at maybe 10-15 mph. Learn how much brake pressure it takes to lock up the rear wheel. Feel the amount of pressure it takes to keep the wheel rolling versus locked up.

- Gradually increase your speed until you can safely brake at 40 mph for the least amount of distance covered. (Make sure you have enough room in the parking lot to safely run at this speed.)

The front brake will become your best friend during wet weather. I know a few people who never use their rear brake in wet weather. They say this will reduce the possibility of locking up the rear wheel and "low siding" the bike down the road. For bikes without ABS brakes this may seem a good strategy if you are not confident in using your rear brake in the rain. In my opinion, relying exclusively on the front brake is not a great idea although I do understand their view point. Without practice, emergency braking without a lock up on a wet road can be a difficult and challenging task to master. However, with practice you can gain complete control of the rear brake and shorten your stopping distances over just using the front brake.

After mastering the effective brake pressure to avoid a rear wheel lock up on dry pavement, practice on a wet surface parking lot. Start at 15 mph again and work your way up to 40 mph.

In wet weather, if you add too much front brake and do not lessen your rear brake pedal force you stand the chance of locking up the rear wheel. This happens because the bike's weight is shifted to the front tire under hard front braking thus lightening or "unloading" the weight on the rear wheel. This may cause a rear tire skid and partially or completely lose traction. Regardless whether you are on a straight away or corner when this happens, you may low side the bike unless you correct it very early.

Correct a slide _very early_ by first lessening the rear brake pedal force while keeping your throttle position. This should allow the rear tire to regain traction and allow the bike to come back in line and stand up. If you completely release the rear brake while in a low slide, you stand the chance of the bike regaining rear tire traction violently and "high siding" the bike. This will launch you off the seat resulting in a lovely bounce and roll down the road. – for you and the bike. Nasty! Just plain NASTY! For more complete information on this subject read Nick Ienatsch's, Sport Riding Techniques and other books.

If you enter a turn with too much speed, practice trail braking and throttle maintenance to scrub off speed and maintain control. Lean forward and push your chin into the turn. In other words, lead with your chin and turn your head to look as far into the turn as possible. In wet weather, this could be the determining factor to successfully or not successfully negotiate a turn.

You should practice your braking and throttle maintenance techniques as often as you can in a local vacant parking lot. Master them on dry pavement and then practice them repeatedly on wet pavement. Not only will you be a better rider, but your comfort level when riding in wet weather will improve dramatically. Your muscles will be more relaxed and you will develop a whole new perspective and level of enjoyment you didn't have before. Rain won't frighten you. You may actually enjoy it and have pride that you, like few others in our sport, can ride comfortably in wet weather. You can now ride wherever and, more importantly, whenever you want.

In Summary:

1. Practice. What more can I say. Practice until you are comfortable and confident that you can stop in the shortest distance possible for any given speed.

The road cleaner passed by here and left this dirt layer on the road. In wet weather this could pose a real concern for the unsuspecting rider. Notice that the road is a different color. That's good **evidence** to slow down immediately. In the rain this will become a slippery mess until washed off.

Chapter 5

Wet Weather Traction

It's mostly about the tires. ***Get ahead with Lincoln*** as the saying goes.

Check your available tire tread depth using a penny if you don't have a tire tread gauge. Put the penny into a tire groove, the top of Lincoln's head first. If you can see over the top of Lincoln's head, replace the tires immediately. Proper disbursement of water is key to having all the available traction possible. Less than a Lincoln's head of tread is placing yourself at a real risk. Being conservative, I use a quarter and Washington's head to measure my tread depth. This is approximately 3/32 deep. I try to change my tires at this depth.

Manufacturers build wear bars into the tread to indicate when to buy new tires. I usually change my tires before these bars come to the surface. My opinion is that life is already too short. Tires are cheap. Death by lost traction is permanent and more expensive than tires for your family. Being penny wise by extending the tire mileage is pound foolish. Replace your tires. It's just smart riding…and living.

Street tires are a compromise of dry versus wet weather traction. However, today's touring and sport tire compounds provide very good road adhesion. If you ride as the skilled, patient, thinking rider you'll have no problems maintaining control during wet weather. All quality motorcycle road tires are made with very good, if not excellent, traction compounds.

Check with your dealer for the recommended tires for your bike. **Buy the best tires you can or can't afford.** They're that important.

Monitor and maintain your correct tire pressures. Under inflated tires allow the tire to overheat and present a real risk of blowout. Properly inflated tires last longer. You will save money in the long run. This should make it easier to buy your next set. Now that's being penny wise.

Some riders advocate lowering tire pressure during wet weather riding. The thought here is to increase the tread footprint to increase traction. This may sound like a good idea but you then have to remember to increase the pressure after you get onto dry pavement. You could be changing pressure a lot during a daily ride. I do not believe that a pressure decrease will afford you a dramatic, if any, increase in traction. I believe it is more important to maintain recommended tire pressures.

Lowering the tire pressure has the potential to shorten a tire's life by overheating it – maybe to the point of failure. Overheating risks escalate when you add a passenger and or luggage weight on an under inflated tire. Decreasing the tire pressure to increase the tire's footprint may increase the risk of hydroplaning since the tire may not cut through water as efficiently as a properly inflated tire. Under inflated tires are not as stable and can produce a wobble in the handling of the bike.

Maintain proper tire pressures. Because of the small air capacity of a typical motorcycle tire, it doesn't take much to critically change the air pressure when the temperature drops. Get into the habit of checking your tire pressure frequently. Either at home or on extended trips, I check my pressures before I start out. This is also a good time to inspect the tire sidewall and tread condition. Look for splits,

Rain Riding Techniques

tears and or a nail. A little time investment here could save hours later sitting on the side of the road.

Maintaining plenty of tire tread is something we can strictly practice. It is one of the best ways to minimize our chances of hydroplaning. Avoiding standing water is a good choice and habit. See what happens when the traffic in front of you enters standing water. You can judge the water's depth by the splash the vehicles produce and make a quick decision to slow down and enter or completely avoid it. You may decide to proceed at a walk's pace. In either case, put on the emergency 4-way flashers, if you have them, or use hand signals to warn traffic around you of your slowed pace.

> **Make it a rule: Before each ride, check your pressure as well as the condition and tread depth of your tires.**

In summary:

1. Check and maintain proper tire pressures at the beginning of each ride and periodically during long trips, especially if there is a big decrease in ambient temperature.

2. Check the tire tread depth. Keep track of your tire mileage and replace when the wear bars have surfaced or sooner. Use Lincoln's or Washington's head as your tread depth tool.

Here is an example of a New England local coastal road. Knowing your riding environment will help you to expect this kind of road hazards and ride accordingly. The beach must not be very far away.

Chapter 6

Highways Versus Byways:

We all know that most accidents occur within 5 miles of the home. "Familiarity breeds contempt" as the saying goes. These neighborhood accidents happen because people are so familiar with their surroundings that they fail to focus on driving. They drive in a self-induced fog. They may be thinking of their upcoming business meeting or the grocery list rather than driving.

Highways and Byways each have their own set of particular hazards. God help you if the driver has a cell phone stuck to their ear. For many, driving and talking on a cell is like patting their stomach and smoothing the top of their heads. Many states have passed laws making it illegal to talk on a cell phone while driving without a hands free attachment because of the dangers they present. Stay very focused on the driving antics of all drivers, and in particular, cell phone users. Plan an escape route in case they decide they like your spot better than their current one. They may even drift between highway lanes or make panic turns without looking to clear surrounding traffic.

Highway Hazards

- Highways and Parkways generally present the least risk of a traffic accident. All traffic is moving in the same direction. You needn't be worried about someone jutting out of an alley or running a red light at an intersection. However, you do have to worry about being in someone's blind spot, being cut off during a lane change or a collision during merging traffic. Being in the merging (wrong) lane becomes especially important during rain when the visibility is decreased for automobile drivers as well as yourself.

- Riding in the highway entry lane or merge lane is the place to avoid. Stay in the left lane of a two lane highway or in the middle and left lanes of a multilane highway. You will have more options in incident avoidance since you will have room to maneuver. Staying in the far right or entry/exit lane is asking to be a target for the person trying to get on or off the highway. They may not see you and if they are in a rush or overly aggressive, they may try to force their way into your slot.

- Watch for the slow pokes. They may not come up to speed while entering a highway. By traveling in the right lane you will have to react to this drastic change in speed. You could become sandwiched between the slowpoke in front of you and the inattentive driver behind you. Why risk it? Move to the left and only use the right lane if you are exiting the highway. Plan an escape route should the driver in front or to the side of you become panicked to exit, brain dead, blind to your existence or inattentive having a cell phone on their ear. Also remember that there are sometimes left side entry and exit ramps. You may encounter slow traffic here as well.

- When traveling during the rain, keep pace with the flow. Certainly, you do not want to be the traffic plug. You'll be asking drivers to tailgate you, leaving you few options in the event of an emergency situation. Keep adequate spacing between you and the vehicle in front. Keep watch of the traffic in front, to the sides and back of you, and **ALWAYS** plan an exit path just in case you get cut off or if there is an accident in front of you. A good rule of thumb is to keep 3 to 6 seconds distance between you and the vehicle in front depending on your speed. This may be difficult because drivers may change lanes in this space. Simply slow down, lengthen your distance and provide yourself more maneuvering options again. Remember, be the patient, thinking rider and anticipate potential problems as best you can. In other words, assume the worst while on the road. It may save your life.

Exit ramps require looking down the road for grease build up at the stop line. Also check out the skid marks here. Skid marks can assist you in grading the steepness of the road for braking purposes as well as accident prone intersections.

During rain do not ride in the center of any lane. This is where all the vehicle oils have accumulated. It will be an area of less and sometimes A LOT LESS traction. Remember to evaluate the condition of the road.

> **Tip: If you are riding the middle lane of a multilane highway, you stand the risk of being attacked from both sides. Stay in the far left lane if you can.**

Byway Hazards

Riding back roads during the rain has its own set of additional associated risks. Of course, some of these can be found on highways too.

- We have to be alert to all sorts of additional traffic and road concerns such as:
    - people pulling out of blind driveways, intersections
    - slow traffic
    - car doors opening
    - dogs and other animals
    - road debris including objects and mud
    - blind corners, potholes, loose sand and gravel wash
- Watch out for dips and underpasses which can flood. Study the car in front of you to gauge a puddle depth and slow down to negotiate this standing water successfully. (By the way, deliberately hydroplaning a motorcycle is not something you want to practice.)
- Drivers running stop lights, stop signs and stop lines.
- Drivers pulling out of parking spaces without looking.

Dirt roads are always a concern for road bikes. Street tires don't provide much purchase on dirt. During the rain these roads can pose a big challenge to negotiate safely. Take your time and stay off large smooth rocks poking up through the surface. They will be slippery. This shot shows a finer example of the dirt roads in New England.

- Slippery road conditions are not always due to rain. Roads in some areas are inherently sandy or gravely, either as a general rule or seasonally.
- Here in the Northeast, each spring, we have road cleanup. Most towns have road cleaning trucks that brush up the sand they spread during winter. Most times this ends up as a caravan of trucks and a traffic nightmare. Cleanup is a good thing since it reduces the need to buy sand for next season. For the motorcyclist, clean up leaves a fine coating of pulverized sand the sweeper truck could not pick up. Hence, we have reduced braking and tire traction. A good clue for this condition is to look for a color change in the road surface. It will generally

have a lighter color - such as very light grey or brown. This color will depend on the type of sand your town uses. Many of these trucks also spray a coating of water to assist in picking up the sand and to keep down the dust. This effectively leaves a very slippery film of mud. The danger presented to the cyclist is usually a BIG surprise. There may be no warning signs that road cleaning is taking place. The cleaning truck may not even be in sight. There maybe 4 or 5 trucks in a line all doing maintenance. This is where your ability to correctly evaluate the road conditions and quick thinking are to your advantage.

- In the spring and fall riders should be aware of tree blossoms and leaves on the roads. These will make the road slippery and tough to navigate in dry weather but worse in the rain. Remember to slow down and proceed with caution. Tree and bush leaves are especially slippery when wet.

Be sure to:

1. Slow down to maximize your available traction.
2. Keep the bike upright and use your throttle and braking techniques to safely traverse the affected road surface.
3. Exit slowly since your tires will have a coating of dirt or mud.
4. Be able to come to a complete stop with in the distance of your view.

In summary - on the Highway:

1. Leave enough space between you and the traffic around you.

2. Don't drive in the center of any lane. Try to ride in the middle or left lanes of a multilane highway staying out of the oil stripe.

3. Plan for and anticipate what the traffic around you is going to do.

4. Anticipate where you need to be to keep out of harm's way

In summary - on the Byway:

1. Anticipate roads hazards like leaves around every blind corner you encounter

2. Check for a road surface color change to anticipate slick spots and hazards.

3. Plan for and anticipate what the traffic around you is going or not going to do.

4. Keep a lookout for potholes and construction obstacles

Always:

1. Leave enough space to maneuver safely in an emergency

2. Plan escape routes

3. Expect the unexpected

4. Be able to come to a complete stop within the distance of your view.

This is not something you'd see in west Texas but will see occasionally in the wooded states of the USA. If you have to pass over it, slow down and try to place yourself as close to 90 degrees to the log (like crossing a railroad track) as you can. Rise off the seat, shifting your weight back over the rear wheel while accelerating a bit to lighten the front wheel. Once the front wheel is over the log, decelerate slightly to shift weight to the front wheel allowing the rear wheel to travel over the log.

Chapter 7

Rush Hour in the Rain

Traveling during rush hour you will have to contend with still more challenges.

1. Watch for rubber banding. Rubber banding is when traffic slows and then moves out repeatedly. Sometimes, rubber banding results in a complete stop. Braking is sometimes rapid and frequent. During wet weather, rubber banding poses braking challenges sometimes greater than any other time while riding a motorcycle. Maintain adequate spacing so you'll not risk locking up your tires during a quick stop. Keep your stops straight and keep the bike upright during hard braking. Keep your head up, looking forward. Do not look down. Try to even out the rubber banding by maintaining an even speed instead of accelerating and braking with the traffic.

2. Keep yourself out of harm's way. I can't say this enough. Anticipate traffic problems and getting painted into the proverbial corner where you have no safe escape. I try to ride in the extreme left lane on highways during rain and in voluminous traffic. I also ride in the right tire track of this lane so cars are less likely to try to invade my space. Riding in the right tire track of the left lane gives me the left lane "leftover" and left shoulder for emergency maneuvers and or a complete evacuation of the lane should the need arise. Caution: Watch for left lane exits and entrances.

3. Change lanes carefully. In the event you have to change lanes while in bumper to bumper or rubber banding traffic, only do so when there is ample room and time to make the change without risking a sudden stop or sudden acceleration. Refrain from abrupt lane changes. Make prodigious use of

your blinker and hand signals. I tend to use both so the other drivers, hopefully, make no mistake about my intentions. I also try to make eye contact but this in no way assures that they have actually seen me.

4. Keep your speed down to lower your stress levels. Afford yourself an escape route and you will lower your risks of an accident.

Remember that truck drivers may have a restricted view directly forward over the large engine hood and radiator as well as expected and known blind spots. Stay to the left side (the driver's side) of the lane if they are directly behind you. They usually have a better view off to this side of their rig.

Use this knowledge to your advantage. By being the patient, thinking rider you will *live long and prosper*.

> **Tip: if your horn is wimpy, check out replacing it with a horn (or two) of 110 decibels or more. They are inexpensive and worth every penny. Get friendly with your horn. Be seen and be heard.**

In summary:

1. Use all the signaling power you have so other drivers will see you,

2. Use all your mirrors and act like an owl – turn your head and look around you.

3. Know where your horn button is without looking and don't be afraid to use it.

4. Ride in the extreme left lane; watch all traffic entering the highway and its effect on the other cars and trucks.

Rain Riding Techniques

5. Try to even out the rubber banding effect by slowing down and driving smoothly.

Notice that part of this road is clear and part has sand and gravel debris. This presents an inconsistent braking surface. This is always a challenge even for the best riders. Slowing down will improve your ability to pass safely. Bikes with an Antilock Brake System (ABS) can provide a significant advantage and safety margin for you.

Chapter 8

To Continue or Stop When the Rain Starts?

Say you are on RT 95 in the Eastern US, in one of the major metropolitan areas - one of the most heavily traveled roads in North America. It hasn't rained for a week. It starts to rain. What do you do? You have a couple of choices:

- Continue to travel knowing the road might have less traction
- Find an overpass or rest area, take a 30 minute break, maybe have a cup of coffee; let the traffic and rain clean much of the slippery mess away, then continue.

Further evaluation of this riding environment and your risks will give more clues for the best choice. Ask yourself:

1. What time of day is it? Nighttime offers reduced vision and increases riding risks.

2. What day of week is it?

- Tired from the weekend activities, the Monday morning traffic is a less attentive crowd than on Wednesday. Everybody seems to be late for work on Mondays.
- Fridays are TGIF. Everybody is in a rush to start the weekend festivities.
- Sundays are travel home days. People are tired, frustrated and impatient with traffic delays.

3. How much traffic is running right now?

Certainly, if it is 5:30 pm (rush hour), raining, and it hasn't rained for 4-5 days, you may want to pull over for an extended period. Let much of this traffic pass. This will clean off much of the oils and grease that have accumulated over the last week. Most importantly, let the commuters who are talking on their cell phones (inattentive), traveling on familiar roads (accident prone), looking through bad wiper blades (can't see well), rehashing their manager's daily criticism (angry and inattentive), making abrupt lane changes to get 1 car length ahead of you (frustrated) proceed. Relax at a rest area or underneath an overpass while having a trail mix bar and a drink of water or soda.

If on the other hand, it's a rainy Sunday morning, traffic is very light and it rained only two days ago, you may decide to keep going. Slow down to maximize your available traction for cornering and braking. Slowing down gives you more time to react to an event on the road. More time gives you more maneuvering and braking options during an emergency. Slowing down and being patient could save your life.

There is an old saying that "speed kills". This is especially true on rainy days. With less speed you'll have more time to evaluate the situation and navigate safely. Having more time gives you more options from which to decide your best course of action.

Maintaining clear vision:

Helmet and glasses fogging in the rain are also something, we have to be concerned with. Many riders crack open their visors to allow air to circulate and reduce the tendency to fog. When fogging starts, wipe your glasses and face shield down with an antifogging agent. You'll ride more safely having done this.

In addition to aerosols and wipes, you may be able to add a secondary visor to help prevent or reduce fogging. These are available by mail order and from your local dealer. Check with them to see what might work best for you.

Some helmets, like my Nolan X-1, allow you to add a secondary visor to the main visor, a visor in a visor setup. This eliminates virtually 98% of fogging. I know this to be true because my wife and I traveled the Blue Ridge Parkway in North Carolina during a violent rain storm. Not finding a safe place to pull over, my wife had to ride with her visor cracked open to prevent fogging. The rain poured down the inside of her visor restricting her visibility even more. Visibility was sometimes less than 10 feet for over 3 miles. This very slow ride was very fatiguing for her and needless to say not very enjoyable. She now plans on carrying antifogging wipes. With my double visor setup, I could see clearly without fogging and therefore rode more safely and relaxed. Until we could safely stop and wait the storm out, I rather enjoyed this surreal but dangerous ride.

Lightning Storms

Because we are not protected by a metal skin as in a car, lightning presents a very real danger to motorcyclists. If lightning is striking in your immediate area – say within 2-4 miles - seek immediate shelter. Preferably, seek inside shelter. Otherwise, find an overpass for protection. Get off your bike and sit a few yards away from it. Try to find dry ground and protection from the storm winds and any flying debris. Never ride into a lightning storm. Lightning storms usually have very heavy rain. The heavy rain may restrict your vision so much that you can't see the road - only the red lights in front of you. Try to anticipate this and act accordingly.

Use common sense. Check out the clouds.

- Do they look really nasty?
- Can you actually see the lightning strikes?
- Has the wind picked up?
- Ask yourself, "Should I really be traveling at this moment? Is my inner voice telling me to get off this road?

A Lightning Storm Lesson:

This past May I was riding to Omaha from Connecticut. It was raining lightly and early evening, around 10 pm. About 80 miles or so east of Kansas City, MO on I-70, I saw the western horizon covered with thick, black, ugly clouds. I could see lightning strikes both vertically and horizontally lighting up the night sky. The rain was really starting to pick up. It was getting difficult to pass the semi's, limited to their 55mph, because of all the tire spray. My inner voice kept telling me to vacate this highway as soon as possible – like NOW! I obeyed that voice and pulled off the first exit and into a Motel 8 for the night. The next morning I found out that not only did KC have one of the worst lightning storms in recent history; they also had 3.5 inches of rain that night. If I had proceeded, I surely would have put myself in harm's way – maybe fatally. The lesson here: Listen to your inner voice… and don't argue!

In summary:

1. Become a patient, thinking, and anticipatory rider.

2. Evaluate conditions, using all road, weather, time, day of the week and traffic clues you have. Then decide what you will do.

Rain Riding Techniques

3. Slow down or maybe stop traveling for a while. Let the roads wash clean of oils.

4. Prepare for helmet fogging if you haven't. Take steps to minimize it by using antifogging agents or use a double visor system.

5. Seek immediate shelter if you encounter lightning and or high winds.

6. Listen to you inner voice. It may keep you safe.

Todd Thompson

Notice the black stripe down the center of each lane. This is the grease groove we find on so any of our interstates and state highways. Ride in the left or right sections (some people call these the tire tracks) of each lane. This will keep you off the most slippery part of the road in the rain. I never ride in the center of a lane even if the sun is shining. The center of each lane also tends to hold solid object debris, increasing the risk of a tire puncture.

Chapter 9

Highway Toll Booths
(and Other Hazardous Things)

Toll booths are notorious for greasy road surfaces. In 1978, I was riding to Cleveland from Washington, DC. Wouldn't you know, it rained all the way. It hadn't rained for almost two weeks. However, traffic was fairly heavy and the highway was reasonably washed clean of oils. Pulling into the "truck lane" toll booth I was in for a big surprise. When I put my feet down to reach for toll change, my feet slid around as if they were on marbles. Luckily my wife, being an experienced passenger, offered no unbalancing movements and we safely made it through the toll.

Since the toll booth lanes are typically covered, they never get rain washed and so the oils accumulate into a very heavy greasy layer. You can see this oily buildup because the road surface is black in color. I would advise staying in the automobile toll lanes, typically the left lanes, and away from the truck lanes, typically the right lanes, if you can.

Better yet, sign up for the electronic toll payment system in your state. Here in the Northeast we use EZPass. The advantage of these electronic toll payment systems is that you can ride straight through without stopping.

However, a few words of caution are needed here:

1. Anticipate that you may have a person without EZ Pass in the wrong lane.

2. Anticipate that you may encounter a person with a broken sensor or person who decides to come to a full stop looking for the green proceed light to change.

3. You may find yourself in a lane that accepts both EZPass and cash. Vehicles in front of you may come to a complete halt. The preference is to avoid these lanes and pass through the EZPass "only" express lanes if they are available.

Be especially careful pulling out of the toll lanes. Your tires may be coated with oil and grease for a brief period of time until they can wash themselves clean. This may take a ¼ mile or more. Jack rabbit starts are not a good idea. Ride smoothly with no abrupt throttle or braking changes until this grease washes off the tires.

> **Tip: Ease on and ease off all controls in the rain. Thinking smoothly will have you executing smoothly. Being smooth, patient and relaxed is what's necessary for safe rain riding.**

Other common road features and weather conditions that you should continually lookout for include:

- Painted areas of the pavement, such as crosswalk hash-marks, large painted letters (like S-L-O-W or LEFT and RIGHT arrows), painted garage floors, or lane lines. Try to drive between the crosswalk lines and letters, stay off the lane indicators as much as possible. These can be slippery. Some towns add a gripping silicate to topcoat the paint, others do not. Go slowly into a garage with a painted floor.

Rain Riding Techniques

- Railroad tracks, and the metal or rubber grating that sometimes surround the tracks, particularly if they are not perpendicular to your direction of travel. Angle your approach to be as close to perpendicular (90 degrees) to the tracks as possible.

- Newly tarred road surfaces. Is there an alternate route you can take? Slow down if not. Road asphalt is a petroleum product and so any oils may float on the surface during a rain until they leach out.

- Slick road surfaces at traffic lights, stop signs and stop lines. Stay away from the center of the lane, where oil and grease have accumulated.

- Accumulated leaves and blossoms. In the fall, accumulated leaves can become slippery layers when rained upon – steer clear and proceed with extreme caution. In the spring blossoms and seed pods may also prove to be slippery during dry and rainy weather.

- Watch out for fog. This not only begets wet road surfaces, but can greatly reduce visibility for you and other drivers. Keep a fierce lookout in front, to the sides and behind you at all times.

- Stay aware of the decreasing temperatures. Freezing temps and precipitation (this includes fog and dew) can cause black ice on the road surface.

- Stay alert to strong and gusty storm winds. These can be life threatening hazards for bikers. Wind blasts can actually push you off the road. Stay aware of strong winds and seek shelter if the wind is minimizing your confidence and safety.

A Decreasing Temperature Lesson:

I have a friend, Jim, who was traveling I 70 east across the Colorado Rockies many years ago. He entered Eisenhower Tunnel up at Vail pass on a rain soaked road. Jim exited the tunnel on his butt with the bike sliding along in front of him. He had hit black ice and lost all traction. (Black ice is a very thin film of ice on the road. You can't see it. Hence, they call it black ice.)

Jim had low sided the bike and sustained no injuries except to his ego. The bike was also not greatly damaged. Luckily, Jim was anticipating a weather and temperature change from one side of the mountain to the other. He had let traffic behind him pass by and he slowed way down to make his way. His riding experience, climate evaluation and judgment saved him from grave injuries. He said that he didn't hurt himself because he stayed slow and relaxed. Yes relaxed, even while sliding down I 70.

Wind can be a real danger on wet roads and bridges. Keep your speed down. This is especially problematic on metal grated bridges. Wet metal surfaces have drastically reduced traction for cars, trucks and particularly, motorcycles. Slow down and increase your bike to vehicle spacing.

A Strong Wind Lesson:

Mr. Herb Gunnison, a man with over 70 years of on and off road motorcycling expertise, wrote to me about a scary rain riding experience he had. I would like share it with you.

"At the beginning of a thunderstorm there are often very high winds. It is prudent to wait until the very high winds abate.

I was traveling in these very high winds, in the rain, in the right lane, not feeling the least bit at risk, when a whopper of a blast hit me. The wind blew me into the left lane of the oncoming traffic. If a car had been coming, I wouldn't be telling you this story. The prudent thing to do is not so much to wait out the storm, but wait out the high winds. If a car had been in that lane, I would have had to take my chances with the bull rushes or whatever was off on the side of the road.

What amazed me about this is that I didn't feel a thing, not even the wind. Here I was toot'ling along with nothing special on my mind and the next thing I know, without swerving, and in a split second, I was riding in the wrong lane.

Strong winds can be lethal in traffic."

Herb's story is a good lesson to remember. Strong winds are even a greater factor on highways that are not bordered by trees or banks to block or dissipate their strength.

In summary:

1. Try not to use truck toll booth lanes.

2. Proceed slowly in and out of toll lanes because of accumulated oils and grease dripping. Be aware that your feet may slip when you put them down too.

3. If you're using electronic toll paying devices, proceed with caution anticipating that the car in front may stop for any number of reasons.

4. Leave the tolls slowly without hard accelerating until your tires have had adequate time to wash themselves clean.

5. Be on the lookout for other road surface hazards that will be slippery wet or dry.

- Painted pavement, traffic arrows, Schools Zone identifiers
- Metal surfaces such as rilroad tracks, bridge grating, metal construction roads plates
- New road asphalt
- Slick surfaces at traffic lights, stop lines, intersections
- Accumulated leaves and blossoms
- Fog
- Decreasing temperatures
- Wind – and potential storm fronts moving in.

Chapter 10

Being Seen / Protective Gear

Traditionally, experienced road riders wore full suits of leather. Today, many riders prefer man made materials like Cordura ™ for their riding garments. These materials can be waterproof, water resistant or full flow thru (mesh) for ventilation cooling in hot weather. These garments typically have protective joint armor built in.

Reflective materials are sewn in to many garments to provide maximum headlight reflectivity during wet weather and darkness. If you tend to layer up like I do, make sure the outer most layer has adequate reflective materials since it will be covering up what you already have on. If the clothing you have purchased doesn't have any, or maybe not enough reflective material, you can always add a reflective orange or lime green colored mesh garment over everything. And they're inexpensive too - typically in the range of $6 - $40 depending on the type. They are easy to find on the Internet. Just search for "reflective vests".

> **Tip: Always wear colorful and reflective clothing and helmets.**
>
> **Be bright and be seen.**

Some riders prefer to ride in full leathers. Most riders would agree that leather is the best protective material you can wrap your body in. But some suits don't have adequate reflective materials sewn on or allow for adequate ventilation when it gets hot. Leather riding suits are not typically waterproof even during the briefest rains. When you purchase this type of garment make sure you add enough reflective materials so people can see you – during the day or night or in wet or dry weather. As mentioned earlier, wearing a florescent safety vest will have other drivers taking notice of you.

Unfortunately, the new owners of a motorcycle may find themselves with no extra money to purchase proper motorcycle clothing. I can't tell you how many times I've seen a rider on a bike with jeans, sneakers, a tee shirt, without gloves and maybe even without a helmet (in those states that don't mandate helmet use). It gives me the willies to think about sliding down the road after "losing it" and making hamburger out of your body. Roads are like a cheese grater on the human body no matter how smooth you think they feel while riding over them. My guess is that jeans will last about 3 seconds or less during a 60 mph slide down a road. Tee shirts? You might as well ride naked! And the rain doesn't make the road surface any softer on your bare skin. You'll just slide a bit further with the same bloody results.

Reflective luggage

A great way to improve wet weather visibility for those behind you is to add reflective tape to your bike luggage or "hard bags". This tape reflects light back to the drivers behind you when their headlights are on. 3m and other manufactures make these reflective tapes and 8x11 sheets. You can find these advertised in magazines and you can find them on the internet by searching for "motorcycle reflective tape".

Other illumination and reflective ideas

All bikes today have federally mandated reflective badges as well as required taillight illumination. If you have purchased an older bike, it may not have front and rear marker side lights or reflective badges. These bikes typically have only the headlight and tail light illuminated. Newer bikes have the blinkers continuously illuminated. These are called running lights. If your bike doesn't have running lights you can buy aftermarket kits to provide this additional safety lighting. It is a worthwhile investment. Some bikes with ABS braking systems monitor the brake and blinker amperage and so you can not add or change to this circuit. Check with your local dealer for the best method to add security and auxiliary lighting products to your particular motorcycle.

I have a reflective smiley face on the rear of my helmet. Drivers tend to notice it and anything that helps to remind them that I'm sharing the road is a good thing.

Adding auxiliary lighting is also a good move. Check with your dealer for more information on what you can safely (electrically) add to your bike.

Remember, that the car and truck drivers also have reduced visibility in the rain. Keep yourself conspicuous to drivers around you. Wear brightly colored and reflective rain gear to increase the odds of being seen by all other drivers on the road.

> **Tip: To help drivers see you, wear a florescent safety vest all the time - in good or bad weather.**

In summary:

1. Always wear protective gear while riding your bike.

2. Make sure your clothing and luggage has ample amounts of reflective materials. Make sure your bike, and you, can be seen adequately from the front, rear, and sides by traffic following you.

3. Frequently check to make sure your headlight (high and low beams), tail light, brake light, blinker bulbs haven't burned out.

4. Check the proper operation of the 4-way emergency flasher.

5. Know and use your hand signals.

6. Add more illumination or reflective materials to you and your bike to improve being seen.

Chapter 11

A Few Quick Words on Clothing

Riding a motorcycle in the rain can be a pleasant experience believe it or not. However, one of the most unpleasant experiences is riding wet and cold in the rain. And it is dangerous for you and those around you.

Whether on long or short rides, you will eventually encounter rain. Make sure you have appropriate clothing to deal with the rain. Your dealer will have a selection of clothing for wet weather riding. Check them out. Also talk to your fellow riders. Interview people at the dealership and ask what they wear. Go on the internet an investigate clothing to suit your needs. Riding in the rain without a face mask or full face helmet is usually either a painful or slow ride.

Clothing comes in all types and configurations. Doing your investigative home work will educate you as to what is going to work best for you, your riding style and riding conditions.

Here is a short and general list of the type of clothing available from various outlets and motorcycle dealers:

> <u>Jackets & Pants</u>: single suit or two piece with breathable lining materials such as Gore-tex™ and its competitors. These should include armor protection pads for the elbows, shoulders, back (spinal), hips and knees.
>
> <u>Rain suits</u>: breathable linings are definitely worth the expense. Usually does not have armor.
>
> <u>Gloves</u>: Leather, textile or leather combo, cowhide, elk, deerskin. Plan on having at least three pairs of gloves: Winter, Rain and Summer.

Heated Clothing: Offered by Aerostitch, Chili, Kreamer, Gerbings, and other manufacturers: vests, jackets, pants, gloves.

Mesh Clothing: including jackets, pants, gloves, and boots. These offer a free flow of air for hot riding conditions but lousy in the rain as you would expect.

Boots: Leather and water proof with breathable liners are the best and are abrasion and burn (exhaust pipes) protective in a crash.

No matter if it is wet and or cold, layering up is the key to riding comfortably. Layering allows you to regulate your body temperature by adding or shedding clothing. Riding in rain can cool the body enough to be pleasant or cause hypothermia. Having the right rain riding clothes can make for a very pleasurable experience. Having the wrong clothing can make for an unpleasant ride or worse.

When it gets cold, I usually add my rain gear as my outside layer, providing a wind block and allowing me to stay warm. Hypothermia is a very real possibility even when it is raining. Remember that hypothermia is an ongoing concern even while riding in 60 degree temperatures.

I once rode to Portsmouth, NH from out west going through Cleveland. It was 37 degrees when I started out and lightly raining. By 10 am or so it warmed to a balmy 47 degrees but at 70 mph the wind chill had me in, effectively, 25 – 30 degree temperatures. Hypothermia was on my mind. I dressed in four layers of clothing. My outer layer was my rain gear (with my safety vest over top). This provided an effective wind block. I made sure I was hydrated by drinking from my water bladder and took plenty of stops to eat and walk about to keep my blood flowing and joints from stiffening.

Outside El Paso, Texas October 2004 I was thinking: "Now where can I quickly and safely stop to put on my rain gear?" In the center of the picture is an obvious rain storm. To the far right you can see another storm behind the telephone poles. I was in for a good soaker. These storms may not last long but you can get very wet in a hurry. Hydroplaning is something to be concerned about since sometimes the water can't flow fast enough off the highway. Knowing that you have lots of tread to disperse the water is comforting.

Chapter 12

Final Thoughts

Learning to competently ride a motorcycle is a lifetime challenge and joy. Safely riding a bike requires that we:

- Develop the proper rider's mindset, behaviors and skills to reducing the risks of an accident - especially in the rain
- Take basic or experienced rider courses to learn or refresh your riding skills.
- Periodically talk to experienced riders about their rain riding techniques and what riding gear works well for them.
- Go to our local school or business parking lot when not being used and practice wet surface braking and throttle techniques.
- Read motorcycle "How to" books. These books can't guarantee to keep us out of harm's way but they can provide insight and lessons to a better, more enjoyable and safer way to ride.

I hope this guide provided valuable information that will increase your motorcycle riding pleasure and safety. Above all, remember to be the patient, thinking and anticipatory rider - regardless of dry or wet weather.

Ride safely and enjoy the rain,

Todd

Todd Thompson

The Cabot Trail, Cape Breton Island, Nova Scotia, July 8, 2004

This is one of North America's motorcycle Meccas. We rode many miles and through lots of rain to get here but, it simply doesn't get any better. On advice from the locals, we ran the trail clockwise for better views. This is looking north east towards Meat Cove, one of my favorite places.